S0-AET-035

John Denver
Man for the World

To Carol Wood Stansfield, teacher, educational innovator, and my wife, whose appreciation for the music of John Denver and for the natural world inspired this work.

Note: Direct quotations from John Denver appearing in this book come from his autobiography, *Take Me Home,* unless otherwise cited.

Cover photograph courtesy johndenver.com.

ISBN: 978-0-86541-088-6
Library of Congress Control Number: 2008925768
Copyright © 2008 John Stansfield. All Rights Reserved.

No part of this publication may be reproduced or transmitted in any form or by any means, electronic or mechanical, including photocopy, recording, or any information storage and retrieval system, without permission in writing from the publisher.

John Denver: Man for the World
Published by
Filter Press, LLC, P.O. Box 95, Palmer Lake, Colorado
719-481-2420 • info@filterpressbooks.com

Printed in the United States of America

John Denver
Man for the World

A NOW YOU KNOW BIO

Number Ten in the Series

John Stansfield

Filter Press, LLC
Palmer Lake, Colorado

Lyrics printed by permission.

Leaving On A Jet Plane
Words and Music by John Denver
Copyright © 1967 Cherry Lane Music Publishing Company, Inc, (ASCAP) and Dimensional Music of 1091 (ASCAP)
Rights for Dimensional Music of 1091 Administered by Cherry Lane Music Publishing Company, Inc.
International Copyright Secured All Rights Reserved

Take Me Home, Country Roads
Words and Music by John Denver, Bill Danoff and Taffy Nivert
Copyright © 1971: Renewed 1999 by Cherry Lane Publishing Company, Inc (ASCAP), Dimensional Music of 1091 (ASCAP), Anna Kate Deutschendorf, Zachary Deutschendorf, Jesse Belle Denver, and Alfred Publishing Company, Inc.
All Rights for Dimensional Music of 1091, Anna Kate Deutschendorf and Zachary Deutschendorf Administered by Cherry Lane Music Publishing Company, Inc, (ASCAP)
All Rights for Jesse Belle Denver Administered by WB Music Corp. (ASCAP)
All Rights for the World excluding the United States Administered by Cherry Lane Music Publishing Company, Inc.
International Copyright Secured All Rights Reserved

Rocky Mountain High
Words and Music by John Denver and Mike Taylor
Copyright © 1972 Cherry Lane Music Publishing Company, Inc, (ASCAP) and Dimensional Music of 1091 (ASCAP) and Alfred Publishing Company, Inc.
Copyright Renewed and Assigned to Anna Kate Deutschendorf, Zachary Deutschendorf and Jesse Belle Denver
All Rights for Dimensional Music of 1091, Anna Kate Deutschendorf and Zachary Deutschendorf Administered by Cherry Lane Music Publishing Company, Inc, (ASCAP)
All Rights for Jesse Belle Denver Administered by WB Music Corp. (ASCAP)
International Copyright Secured All Rights Reserved

On The Wings Of A Dream
Words and Music by John Denver
Copyright © 1983 Cherry Lane Music Publishing Company, Inc, (ASCAP) and Dimensional Music of 1091 (ASCAP)
Worldwide Rights for Dimensional Music of 1091 Administered by Cherry Lane Music Publishing Company, Inc.
International Copyright Secured All Rights Reserved

Flying For Me
Words and Music by John Denver
Copyright © 1986 Cherry Lane Music Publishing Company, Inc, (ASCAP) and Dimensional Music of 1091 (ASCAP)
Worldwide Rights for Dimensional Music of 1091 Administered by Cherry Lane Music Publishing Company, Inc.
International Copyright Secured All Rights Reserved

Contents

1 Life on the Move

"You're a brat." Being called a brat might offend some people, but not young Henry John Deutschendorf. In his case, he knew it did not mean a kid with bad behavior. The boy, later known as John Denver, was simply an Air Force "brat," a child of a military family. His dad, an officer, flew jets for the United States Air Force.

Being a military brat usually means moving a lot. Parents get stationed at various military bases all over the country and around the world. Their children often move with them. John and his younger brother, Ron, were no different.

Henry John Deutschendorf Jr. was born December 31, 1943, in New Mexico, where his father was stationed at Roswell Army Air Station. His parents,

Henry John Sr. (known as Dutch) and Erma (whose maiden name was Swope), came from Oklahoma.

When he was two, young John and his mother lived in Tulsa with her family for a year. At that time, Dutch served on the Marshall Islands in the Pacific, piloting planes making aerial surveys as part of nuclear bomb testing. The family next transferred to Japan, where Ron was born and John started school, at a younger age than most of his classmates.

Tucson, Arizona, was the place John lived the longest while growing up. After seven years there and one year in Montgomery, Alabama, the family transferred to Fort Worth, Texas, where John finished high school. "I never felt that I had a home," he once told an interviewer.

"In Tucson, I was the painfully shy Deutschendorf son," John recalled. "From six to thirteen, I was pretty much a loner." Moving twice more as a teenager made life no easier for the insecure, emotionally sensitive boy. "I had to go from newcomer to some form of acceptance in each of these communities."

Military brats and others who often move develop ways to deal with forever being the "new kid on the block." They try making flashy first impressions. Or they stay silent, blending in to the wallpaper. Some make acquaintances but avoid deep friendships. Some

Courtesy johndenver.com

Erma, Dutch, and John pose in a portrait taken near the end of World War II.

search for only one good friend in each place they live. Others get noticed by fighting. John Deutschendorf was not flashy or loud. Fighting he avoided at all costs. "Maybe I was a physical coward," he said, "but I always tried to talk my way out of fights." His nonviolent strategy usually worked. Even so, the upset of conflict churned inside him after confrontations.

Born to Climb

Growing up before the days of artificial climbing walls, John would climb rocks, trees, houses—just about anything. In Arizona, his father sometimes took him to the Tucson Mountains, where the boy scrambled like a lizard over rough-faced boulders. But what goes up must come down. Jumping off a roof he had climbed, John broke his arm—for the second time in two months.

To some, the Sonoran desert on the edge of Tucson appears as friendly as a coiled rattlesnake. Young John Deutschendorf liked it, though. He liked rambling up rocky desert hills and down bone-dry washes. After school, he rode his bike three blocks from his family home. Where the city streets ended, the desert wilderness began.

With his few friends or alone, John re-created in his play the ancient history he learned about in school. He imagined sword-wearing Spanish conquistadors marching along the horizon. Stick shelters became forts or castles. Empty streambeds were rivers roaring through mountain canyons. Cowboys and Indians appeared and disappeared in the desert wind.

Three eucalyptus trees, much taller than the thorny desert scrub, grew in a yard near the Deutchendorf's house. John often climbed them and bounced on springy branches at the top. Sometimes he sat quietly with a bird's-eye view of city and desert, imagining his future.

One day, aloft in one of the trees, John dreamed of a home high in the mountains. It would be a place where people could meet, talk, make friends, and not be alone. As he grew, John held fast to that vision. Years later, he found a mountain valley where the dream could be shaped into reality.

Musical Kid

Despite all the moves, John found a way to win friends in new places. "Music is what opened the door for me," he told an interviewer. "I can't remember not singing. Evidently from the time I could first talk, I started repeating the songs I heard on the radio. They called me 'jitterbug.' That was the popular music form at the time."

His mother and grandmother encouraged John's musical talents. Erma enrolled him in the Tucson Boy's Chorus. He also sang in the choir of the Presbyterian church his family attended.

When he was 12, John's Grandmother Swope showed him a Gibson guitar she had played in her younger days. As she later recalled, "I got the guitar out and let him pick around on it. He just tried to sing up a storm. And I said, 'John, would you practice if Mama gave you music lessons?' He asked his Mama and she said, 'If you will practice.' So I gave him the guitar." John practiced often and started writing songs.

In 1957 at his new school in Montgomery, Alabama, John joined the boy's chorus. The teacher learned that he played guitar and wrote songs. She asked him to bring his instrument to school. The decision to "come out of hiding" with his music was difficult for the shy boy. For the class later that week, he performed a song that he had written called "Lazy Little Stream." Then he sang a few songs popular on the radio. Soon kids recognized John in the halls. Despite gaining school friends, he found living in Montgomery "a grim prospect."

Segregation disturbed John's growing sense of fairness and **equality**. It "went against everything in my education that meant something to me," he stated. "In Tucson I went to school with a racially varied bunch of kids." He strongly disliked the attitude in Montgomery of "us against them," which said "nothing about us joining with them to make the world a better place." He was becoming, in his words, a **social activist**. He always rooted for the underdog.

Story Behind the Song
As a grown-up, John wrote "This Old Guitar," a song about the many gifts Grandmother Swope's guitar provided. He recorded it on his 1974 *Back Home Again* album.

Military Regimen

In 1958, the family moved again. This time to Carswell Air Force Base in Fort Worth, Texas. Dutch rose to the

Know More!

Birth of a Movement

When the Deutschendorfs arrived in Montgomery in 1957, they found the city alive with tensions between black and white community members. Schools, housing, churches, restaurants, hotels, drinking fountains, restrooms, even sections on the city buses were separated by race. In November 1956, the United States Supreme Court outlawed segregation. For years after, despite the changes in law, many places kept the racial barriers.

In December 1955, an African American woman, Rosa Parks, was arrested because she refused to surrender her seat in the white section of a Montgomery bus. In response, black citizens **boycotted** the bus system for a year. The Reverend Martin Luther King Jr. led the bus boycott and other nonviolent community protests against discrimination. Those actions and others elsewhere touched off the struggle for racial equality known as the American Civil Rights Movement.

rank of lieutenant colonel and became commander of a squadron of B-58 Hustler bomber aircraft. Flying the supersonic B-58 required experience and great concentration. Dutch set a world speed record in the plane while stationed at Carswell. As a flight instructor, he taught pilots the complex skills of jet aviation.

In the U.S. Armed Forces, two important parts of **military regimen** must be followed—regulations and orders. Regulations are written "rules of the game" describing how military life must be conducted. Orders, commands for action that must be obeyed, flow from higher-ranking to lower-ranking personnel.

As a career Air Force officer, Dutch lived a life dictated by orders and regulations. Like many military people, his home life was also orderly and regulated. Erma saw to that. She kept the house clean, neat, and well stocked with food. She tried to keep the boys that way, too. And, Dutch confided in a magazine interview, "I admit I was kind of rough on the kids."

The military lifestyle rankled John. The older he got, the more he struggled with his parents' regimen, especially that of his father. "We started to not get along," John observed. "I thought he was pretty hard on me about a lot of things. He would hassle me about things he wanted done, and ridicule me if I didn't come up to snuff. I resented all this." John grew frustrated, unable to share his ideas and feelings with his parents. Instead, he bottled them up inside.

John faced more responsibilities and stricter discipline than his younger brother. Once he complained to an interviewer that Dutch never called him by name, just "Hey, boy." In time, John learned what his father already knew: being the oldest girl or boy in a family can be difficult. Dutch grew up the oldest of ten brothers, working hard on an Oklahoma farm while attending school. Dutch's older (and only) sister, Anne, had plenty of family responsibilities, as well.

An Emotional Roller Coaster Ride

That was what John's high school years amounted to. He was a good student. He went out for football one year, hoping to get noticed at Fort Worth's Arlington Heights High School. But he disliked the physical hammering he took and only got to play in one game all season.

As in Tucson and Montgomery, making friends at school proved difficult. Friendship was easier at the senior fellowship, a church group that met Sunday nights. The teenagers prayed, danced, played games, or just talked. John sometimes played guitar and sang.

By sophomore year, word about John's music began to spread, even at school. "I got together with a couple of bands and started playing parties, proms," he said in a magazine interview. Music "was the thing I always did

John at fourteen, sports a late 1950s
flattop haircut.

Courtesy johndenver.com

that was easy and made me feel good. I liked singing for people."

Dutch wanted John to know his Oklahoma roots and relatives and the work of farming. He sent his fourteen-year-old son to help with the wheat harvest on a friend's farm. John made $1.00 an hour driving a tractor, and he loved the job. Each summer, he looked forward to getting away from Fort Worth to work the harvest.

The summer after his junior year, John got a call from his uncle Dean that changed his life. Dean was Dutch's second-youngest brother and was only a few years older than John. He hired John to drive a truck for his work crew.

Dean Deutschendorf was a positive, in-charge, and energetic person. He presented his nephew an excellent role model. As John stated, "He took me under his wing, like I was his kid brother. The world looked great when I was around Dean. I started to get a picture of who I would like to be, a happy person who made other people feel good."

Back in Fort Worth, John tried to match Dean's upbeat nature. But his home and school situations had not really changed. Then, that winter, Dean died in an auto accident. John grew depressed and withdrawn. He stumbled through daily life like a robot. He retreated to his room, played guitar, and spoke little to anyone. He called himself "Mr. Serious" and "a dot: round and flat without edges or depth. That's how I felt and that's what I thought others saw."

John was not very popular with girls and did not date often. One Friday night in his senior year, he came out of his shell enough to make a date. But after work that evening, Dutch went to the officer's club to drink beer with friends. He forgot that John needed the car. The date had to be canceled. Dutch never apologized after coming home late. Erma erupted in anger. She threatened to leave Dutch, who only laughed at her suggestion. John had not heard his parents argue this way before.

As John recalled in an interview, "Things weren't right and I felt responsible for it and felt that I should just leave." Early the next morning, John called the variety store where he worked part-time, saying he had to leave town due to a family emergency. He packed his guitar, drawing board, and a suitcase in the family's 1950 Mercury and headed for Los Angeles, California. Driving west, visions of freedom and a hazy, but exciting future danced in his head.

Erma and Dutch never intended to break up, and they were very worried about John. Dutch flew a jet over highways leading to Oklahoma and points west, but never spotted the car. Erma called former neighbors in Tucson and just missed John, who had stayed with them the night before.

Almost broke, John called home from L.A., seeking the address of old friends Carl and Nina Hart, with whom he hoped to stay. Dutch offered to fly out and drive back with John to Fort Worth. John agreed. "When I got there," Dutch recalled for a magazine article, "the look out of his eyes was animal. He was scared to death."

John ended the story of his runaway this way: "Driving back across the country, he tried to talk to me, to put things straight and air out all of the hard feelings, but I don't think he knew how to have that conversation, and I didn't help much. But of course, beyond my resentments, I knew he cared."

East of Tucson in a region of knobby hills, Dutch stopped the car. He waited silently for a long time while John climbed rocks, just as he had when he was a boy. Even without Dutch saying a word, John understood that his father forgave him for running away. John knew that letting him climb "was our coded way in which he spoke to me."

2 The Folk House

Driving John to college in the fall of 1961, his father told him: "You've got a musical talent that many people don't have. But that doesn't make you better than anybody else." Dutch rarely offered his son advice. John took the blunt words positively to heart. "He was acknowledging my ability," John said, "but he didn't want me to get too big for my britches."

John knew his parents expected him to attend college after he graduated from high school. He considered the Air Force Academy, but poor eyesight prevented him from becoming an Air Force pilot like his dad. John decided on Texas Tech University in Lubbock, where an **architecture** program sounded interesting. His parents did not support his studying music.

The freshman found college life "awfully exciting." On his own, he could study—or not study—when he wanted, play guitar for other students or alone, and go to bed when he wanted. Popular as the dorm **troubadour**, John found that making friends became easier and more natural.

What made John most happy and kept him in school was "the music I was making, and sometimes getting paid for. I sang with a group called the Alpine Trio and sometimes I sang by myself." His view of himself as "Mr. Serious" changed. "I think during that period I was trying to lighten up a little."

Events in the fall of 1963 rocked the United States. On November 22, an assassin shot President John F. Kennedy in Dallas, Texas. The entire nation and much of the world mourned the popular leader. Many Texans struggled with grief and guilt over the horror that had happened in their state. John shared their feelings and wrestled with demons of his own. His grades were poor, and he was torn between music and school.

During Christmas break 1963, John traveled to the Deutschendorf's new house in Florida, hoping they might help him plan his future. It did not turn out that way. His parents fretted over John's poor grades. "I was very tense and Dad and I were at each other's throats," he confessed.

For John, back at school, it was either make good

grades on semester exams or quit school to explore the music world. His poor grades told the tale. John wrote his parents about leaving school. Dutch wrote back. As John described the letter, "He chewed me out pretty good for what I was doing. But then he said: If that's what you have to do, then you should do it." Enclosed was a check for $250. John concluded, "I may never have experienced a more profound expression of my father's love and concern."

New Kid in Town

John Deutschendorf, just turned 20 in December 1963, did not run away *from* Texas as he had in high school. After leaving college, he ran *to* Los Angeles, intending to learn everything possible about the music business. The L.A. area hummed like a beehive with musical activity. **Folk music** was very popular at that time. It was the kind of music John wanted to perform.

Driving into the city, John drove by a building marked with three huge letters, RCA. Here he was, fresh from Lubbock, Texas, passing the home of RCA Records, the company that recorded Elvis Presley, Paul Anka, and many other music stars. Maybe someday, he thought, I will sing for RCA, too.

In Los Angeles, family friends Carl and Nina Hart offered John a place to stay. Carl, a civil engineer, gave him a day job as a **draftsman**. At night, John followed the music, performing at open stages, where anybody could sign up to play, and meeting other young folk musicians.

On his second Sunday in town, he signed up for the open stage (called a **hootenanny**) at the Back Porch, part of a club called Ledbetter's. Randy Sparks, Ledbetter's owner, liked John's voice. Sparks hired him as the opening act for the featured band, the Back Porch Majority. John performed a 20-minute song set for each show from Tuesday through Saturday nights for $100 a week.

Somewhere in someone's basement or dusty attic, there is an audiotape of John's performances the first week at Ledbetter's. That tape, John admitted in an interview, proves that he went from being really terrible to only pretty bad in just five days. He had nowhere to go but up.

L.A. Apprenticeship

When Sparks hired John, he also made him two other offers, both eagerly accepted. One was the chance to make a studio recording of a few songs, called a demo, for use in promoting his work to clubs and record companies. The other was a place to live rent-free at a house Randy owned called the Folk House.

Members of the Back Porch Majority lived at the Folk House, a three-bedroom suburban bungalow. Danny Dalton, the leader of the Majority, taught John about stage presence. "It was he," John said, "who got me to think about what I wore on stage, about my **patter** with the audience, and even whether my hair was combed or not."

Another housemate was Mike Crowley, an expert musician. He mentored John on guitar technique and taught him to play a twelve-string guitar. (A standard guitar has six strings.) All the folk singers shared songs with each other. Sparks, also leader of the popular folk group The New Christy Minstrels, introduced John to the business end of making music.

In spring 1964, Dutch came to California on a military assignment. He attended shows at Ledbetter's and visited the Folk House. Dutch observed details of his son's new life without saying much, though he seemed impressed. John hoped that "he was going to go home and tell Mom that she didn't have to worry about John."

John quit his day job and concentrated on music. "Except for working at the club," he said, "I spent all my time in the house—shy and reclusive as always—learning songs." Being on stage helped him overcome shyness. Performing, he learned, was a two-way street. If he shared his music and his emotions with the audience, he sometimes received an energizing feeling of encouragement from them in return.

After early success at Ledbetter's, John signed a contract to appear there for twenty-six more weeks. On Sundays, he ran Ledbetter's hootenanny. On Mondays, his night off, he headed for the Troubadour, L.A.'s top music club. The club featured expert performers for him to listen to, study carefully, and learn from.

During this period in L.A., the only constant about the music scene was change. Folk groups and rock bands came together, changed members, and broke up. Groups with new names formed out of the wreckage of old ones. Bands experimented with all kinds of music. Even solo performer John Deutschendorf toyed with the idea of joining a band.

Through a friend, John met Jim McGuinn, a guitarist who had played with a well-known folk group, the Chad Mitchell Trio. Shy but very ambitious, McGuinn wanted to form an American band that

Know More!

Musical Tsunami

Music exploded in the United States and other countries during the 1960s. A decade earlier, rock and roll grew from several styles of popular music, particularly swing, blues, and country. Rock appealed to teenagers, with Elvis Presley its biggest star. More traditional music forms, folk and blues, were extremely popular from about 1955 to 1965. Young people, especially on college campuses and in cities, were exploring their musical and personal roots during the folk music revival.

The "British Invasion" of the mid-1960s reshaped the face of rock and roll. The Beatles, Rolling Stones, and other English bands achieved worldwide fame and huge record sales, often playing music with American roots. John Deutschendorf listened well to their music. He was excited when British rockers played the Troubadour. Musical creativity and innovation rolled like a tsunami from continent to continent around the world throughout the decade.

played folk and rock music with vocal **harmony** similar to the Beatles. John sang several times with McGuinn, Gene Clark, and David Crosby. The aggressive and outspoken Crosby clashed with the reserved and innocent Deutschendorf. John decided to stay a solo act.

Jim (later known as Roger) McGuinn's band took the name the Byrds. They popularized the blends of music called folk-rock and, later, country-rock. From 1965 to 1968, the Byrds had several hit records, challenging the Beatles for top record sales.

Randy Sparks urged John to adopt a simpler, catchier stage name than Deutschendorf. The club owner told him his name would not fit on a record label. After rejecting several suggestions, John noted matter-of-factly, "I chose Denver, which I associated with the Rocky Mountains."

Hitting the Road

Driving his new blue Ford Mustang convertible, up-and-coming musician John Denver headed for Florida to visit his family in December 1964 with lots on his mind. His musical skills and confidence had grown during the past year. He supported himself financially. Music clubs in other cities showed interest in hiring him. Most important, as a performer John was his own man, never interested, as others were, in imitating someone else's music.

At home, though, John Deutschendorf was still

just his father's oldest son. As the visit wore on, John argued with Dutch over just about everything. The time at home was no fun.

"On the other hand," John proudly stated, "the club date I got myself on the way back in Houston, at the Jester, where I performed just after Christmas, was a bit of a triumph." His engagement there was extended from two weeks to four weeks by popular demand. At the club, John met the famous folk group, the Kingston Trio, who praised his work.

Back in L.A., in singer Bob Dylan's words, "the times were a-changin.'" And a-changin' fast.

Folk music bands added drummers and traded in their **acoustic** instruments for electric ones. Folk hootenannies turned into open stages for aspiring rock bands. The number of clubs featuring folk music shrank rapidly.

Worst of all, Randy Sparks was losing interest in John's performances. The club owner did not renew Denver's contract with Ledbetter's. Possibilities died for a record deal they had discussed.

"The Sixties were moving on and I was missing them," John later said.

Looking back on his time at Ledbetter's, however, Denver concluded in a magazine interview, "I was given

Courtesy johndenver.com

John Denver seems to gaze toward the future in a photo from early in his career.

the great opportunity to find out what I wanted to do, what worked and what didn't on stage, and I found out who I was as a performer."

Instead of sadly moping around L.A., John found a new locale where people wanted to hear his music. Reaching out to audiences in new places became a strategy he depended on throughout his career.

The Lumber Mill club in Scottsdale, Arizona, hired John Denver—with his six-string guitar, loud twelve-string guitar, and booming eighteen-string guitar—to perform during spring and summer 1965. At the club, he made an important connection. He met Mike Kirkland of the nationally known folk group, the Brothers Four. Kirkland knew that his record producer, Milt Okun, was hunting for a singer to replace Chad Mitchell in the vocal group. At Kirkland's suggestion, John mailed Okun a demo tape of his music.

More than 200 singers sent Okun demos. To John's surprise, he was invited to New York to audition. He later told a magazine interviewer, "I had a cold. At the first audition I tried to sing like Chad [in a high **tenor** voice] and just did *terrible*. [At trio member] Joe Frazier's house, I learned two songs. We went back to Milt Okun's office with Joe singing with me and it was a whole different thing. They said, 'Don't call us, we'll call you.'"

John did not know it, but he had already earned Okun's vote. Okun stated in an interview, "When John first walked into the audition with a smile as wide as his face, I was won over completely." A few days later, Okun called John in Arizona and offered him the job.

John, Joe Frazier, and Mike Kobluk rehearsed for only six days before the renamed Mitchell Trio debuted at the famous Cellar Door club in Washington, D.C. Denver confessed that, with the trio, he "stepped beyond the charted territory" he had known before.

The Mitchell Trio—Mike Kobluk (left), John Denver, and Joe Frazier— sang together for four years.

Story Behind the Song
"The Ballad of Spiro Agnew," a satire from Denver's Mitchell Trio days, appeared on his first solo album, *Rhymes and Reasons.* The song pokes fun at the U.S. vice president who resigned in 1973 while under investigation for taking **bribes** from businesses.

The group's established musical **repertoire** of folk, funny, poetic, and **protest songs** made John's transition easier. The newcomer enjoyed the group's **satire**. These songs make audiences laugh at crazy things people and governments sometimes do, like building life-destroying nuclear weapons and saying they keep people safe.

"It was from the trio and most specifically Joe Frazier," John said in an interview, "that I started becoming more socially and politically aware of what was going on in the country in regard to **civil rights** and government." That included the war in Vietnam. The trio played at pro–civil rights rallies and marched in antiwar demonstrations.

The growing U.S. military involvement in Vietnam sparked fiery national debate. Despite his Air Force upbringing, John firmly believed that U.S. participation in the war was wrong. It felt right to sing about changes needed in America. However, he said, "I wasn't used to seeing myself as a rabble-rouser. Parents [of soldiers] would come up after the show full of anger about what we had done on stage. I didn't know how to talk to these people."

John Denver brought musical gifts to the Mitchell Trio—a dynamic voice, solid guitar playing, a lively presence on stage, and new songs from his repertoire. Soon after joining, he experienced for the first time the full process of making a record. The album was titled *That's the Way It's Gonna Be*. Though it was not an RCA record, as he imagined a year earlier, it was a landmark in his young career. John Denver's musical education was progressing at a rocket's pace.

3 Playing Solo, Being Married

Often energizing. Sometimes frustrating. Always educational. John Denver's stint with the Mitchell Trio included all three experiences. He traveled the country with the group for three years, playing colleges, community halls, festivals, and clubs. Along the way, he met many of his favorite singers and songwriters. Audiences responded enthusiastically to the trio's music. They recorded three creative and entertaining albums, which included several songs John wrote.

A few days after writing "Leaving on a Jet Plane," John played it for Milt Okun at the Philadelphia Folk Festival, where the Mitchell Trio performed. The producer loved it. That fall while in L.A., John recorded the song and a dozen more on an untitled album to give to friends and family at Christmas.

Know More!

Songwriting—Making Music Magic

John Denver often said that songs found him without his looking for them. For a songwriter, the inspiration for a song may creep in like a turtle or strike like lightning. Sometimes the words or lyrics, written as a poem, come first. Or a melody rambles around awhile in the brain, looking to partner up with words. However a song emerges, songwriting combines words and music in a magical, creative mix never before heard.

John made sure to get a copy of the album to Peter, Paul, and Mary, America's most popular folk group, whose records Okun produced. Early in 1967, the group recorded "Leaving on a Jet Plane." It rose slowly on the national record sales charts, finally climbing to number one in 1969. It became the group's biggest hit song. The name of songwriter John Denver began to spread through the music world.

Denver knew some good times with the trio. He also experienced bad times. The group never made enough money. Traveling by jet, living on the road costs a lot. In the late 1960s, rock and roll ruled the music world. Audiences dwindled for folk music shows. The trio's records sold poorly.

Story Behind the Song

The birth of Denver's first popular song, "Leaving on a Jet Plane," presents a fine example of the songwriting process in action.

On a quiet Virginia summer night in 1966, John Denver, between tour dates, worked on an oil painting. He'd developed an interest in painting while studying architecture. Growing hungry, he put down paint brush and palette. A sandwich and cold beer tasted good.

Then, he said, "I picked up my guitar and wrote a song with my soul wide open and my mind picturing the scene as if it stood before me, real enough to touch." He wrote:

> *All my bags are packed*
> *I'm ready to go*
> *I'm standing here outside your door*
> *I hate to wake you up to say goodbye...*
> *'Cause I'm leavin' on a jet plane*
> *Don't know when I'll be back again*
> *Oh, babe, I hate to go*

At the time he wrote the song, John had no special someone to bid a sad good-bye, no one to greet joyously upon returning. He just knew he wanted a special person like that in his life. Songs came to him like gifts, John believed, when he was in the "right space" to receive them.

During the Cellar Door engagement in 1965, John's weekly pay and hotel costs each equaled about $250, leaving his pockets empty. During what was supposed to be a 1967 European tour, several concerts were cancelled. In the end, the trio performed only one paying concert.

According to the group's financial manager, Hal Thau, the group owed more than $40,000. Thau advised the singers to disband and walk away from the debt. John had other ideas: "I felt strongly that honoring our debt was the right—the only—thing to do." Bravely, stubbornly, a little at a time, he paid off what the trio owed. To raise money, John picked up occasional solo jobs, when not busy with the group.

The trio struggled on. After seven years of touring, Joe Frazier, restless for greener pastures, left the trio in the fall of 1967. Texas singer David Boise took his place. A string of managers and booking agents came and went. Mike Kobluk retired in 1968. With no original members left, Denver, Boise, and newest member Mike Johnson lost the right to use the Mitchell Trio name. The group broke up in early 1969.

Hal Thau believed in John's musical future. He volunteered to be the singer's financial manager, even though "there were no finances to manage" at the

The voices of the Mitchell Trio blend in close
harmony as they sing for a concert audience.

time. Another believer was record producer Milt
Okun, who offered John musical coaching, and looked
for a company to record him. Okun, Thau, and
Denver remained business associates and close friends
for decades.

Ann Martell

The Mitchell Trio presented a concert at Gustavus Adolphus College in St. Peter, Minnesota, in spring 1966. After the show, students invited the singers to a charity fund-raiser. A girl with long brown hair, wearing jeans and a flannel shirt, came onstage with a sign announcing each act. John's reaction was immediate: "She filled me with wonder. I could feel love on the wing."

After the fund-raiser, someone with a guitar asked John to sing some songs. The brown-haired girl sat right in front. John directed every song her way. When the singing was done, he asked her name and where she was from. She was a hometown girl named Ann Martell.

When the trio returned to southern Minnesota for fall concerts, John called Ann. She remembered him and accepted an invitation to the concert in nearby Mankato. The following Saturday, John met Norma and Jim Martell, Ann's parents. From that weekend on, John confided, "Our **courtship** began to flourish."

John spent part of the Christmas holidays that year getting to know the Martells, including Ann's two sisters and her brother. The family's well-mannered guest bubbled with high spirits, perhaps trying hard to win their friendship. According to John, Annie never seemed to need approval. Pretty and very popular, she had lived and grown up in the same place all through childhood. She appeared a self-assured person. In that quality, Annie and John were opposites. Her assurance attracted him.

That winter, Annie and other students from Gustavus Adolphus traveled to Aspen, Colorado, to ski. John showed up in the scenic mountain town to surprise her. Neither of them could have guessed then how important Aspen would become to their lives.

Maintaining a love affair proved difficult with John frequently on the road. On the phone from faraway places, John asked Annie to marry him two times before she agreed. The couple married June 9, 1967, at the Lutheran church in St. Peter. The Deutschendorf family, Grandmother Swope, the Martell family, and many from the local community attended the big wedding. Mike Kobluk, David Boise, and other musicians performed at the event.

In late summer, the young newlyweds flew to Italy to experience art, architecture, and life together. "We did have a good time," John commented. Then the Mitchell Trio met in England for the "European tour"

*John and Annie Denver celebrate with friends at a party
shortly after their marriage.*

that in the end, resulted in only one concert. Annie,
perhaps discouraged by the tour's failure or just home-

sick, returned to America. As she told an interviewer about their early marriage, "John and I really didn't know each other." John, his emotions knotted up inside, said he "couldn't tell her how much I needed her. I took it as a kind of abandonment." Years later, he said, "I still hit myself for letting her go off."

Making Moves on His Own

After the trio's breakup in 1969, performing solo again felt good. John got a two-week **gig** in Snowmass, near Aspen, that winter. The two weeks turned into two months spread over the ski season. That was followed by a month at a club in San Francisco and college coffeehouses here and there.

Advertised as "the writer of 'Leaving on a Jet Plane' and formerly of the Mitchell Trio," John Denver was in no way famous. An Aspen friend, Paul Lurch, told a magazine, "None of us believed John Denver was going to be a household [name] in 1968, but John Denver did. Even when he was poor, he was an incredible optimist."

In John's confident words: "I was convinced that one day we were going to live in the mountains. People were going to listen to what I had to say, and what I had to say to people would be meaningful. Annie took it all with a grain of salt, as well she might."

Annie and John lived on a shoestring budget, first in Chicago, then in Minneapolis. "It was hand-to-mouth and day-to-day and no fun," John said in an interview. For a while, they owned only one lamp, which they moved from room to room for light.

After many attempts, Milt Okun secured a recording contract for John in the summer of 1969. RCA Records, the company John dreamed about, signed him for two albums a year over two years. He received $7,000 in advance for each record. Elated, John said, "Suddenly a solution had arisen for our money problems."

The number-one hit, "Leaving on a Jet Plane," and three other original songs appeared on the first album, *Rhymes and Reasons*. The record also included satirical songs he performed with the Mitchell Trio and "When I'm Sixty-Four," a humorous Beatles song. Not many people bought the first album or the two that followed. Radio stations did not play John's songs much either.

In those days, two things worked together to turn musical recordings into hits—radio airplay and record sales. People heard a song they liked on the radio and went to a record store to buy it. They either bought the

Courtesy johndenver.com

Two of John's trademarks, round granny glasses and a big
smile, stand out in this photo from the early 1970s.

song as a single, a small vinyl plastic disk with one tune on each side, or an album, a bigger, double-sided collection of a dozen or so songs. Magazines, such as *Billboard*, kept close track of record sales on numbered lists called charts.

A Mountain of Plastic Platters

The night after Christmas 1970, John Denver began his first stint as solo **headliner** for the Cellar Door in Washington. His friends Bill and Taffy Danoff provided the opening act. After a successful show that week, Annie, John, and other musicians headed to the Danoff's apartment to make more music. Despite a broken thumb from a minor auto accident on the way, John was raring to sing when they reached the apartment well after midnight.

"Bill and Taffy showed me this [unfinished] song they were writing called 'Country Roads,'" John recounted for a magazine, "and I flipped over that song. That morning we finished writing the song and I said we've got to record this on my next album, which was *Poems, Prayers, and Promises*."

The following night at the Cellar Door, the three

musicians premiered their new creation, singing:
Almost heaven, West Virginia
Blue Ridge Mountains, Shenandoah River
Life is old there, older than the trees
Younger than the mountains, growing like a breeze
Country Roads, take me home…

When they finished, the audience went crazy, standing and applauding for five minutes.

With the release of the "Country Roads" single and the *Poems, Prayers, and Promises* album in 1971, sales of the records went through the roof. John's music was frequently heard on radio stations nationwide. His name and smiling face began to appear in newspapers and on television.

Take Me Home

Like prospectors before them, many young people during the 1970s discovered the natural splendor of Colorado. Some came, enjoyed the visit, and left. Many others stayed to make it their home.

Late in 1970, Annie and John returned to the Colorado mountain valley they both loved. "We pulled into Aspen," Annie recalled in an interview. "It was a great time. I thought, oh my gosh, we're really home." For years, she and John had talked of buying a home in the mountains.

With money in the bank from **royalties** for "Leaving on a Jet Plane," they shopped for a house. Everything they saw cost too much. Aspen was—and is—a very expensive place to live. A friend suggested they just buy land. He showed them a hilltop lot in the Starwood subdivision outside of town. John reflected on that moment: "I looked out over the valley. I knew we'd found home. We'd stumbled on it, but I'm convinced it was preordained that we'd find this place."

The couple bought the lot. It took all the money they had. They rented a place in town. For a year, John, the former architecture student, waited impatiently to construct the house he had been building in his head for so long.

A year later, with royalties from "Country Roads" rolling in, they built their house overlooking the Roaring Fork River valley and the peaks beyond. John Denver had finally found a permanent home.

Story Behind the Song
Not long after moving to Aspen, John climbed on to a ski lift headed up a mountainside. In an instant, images from nature filled his senses and imagination. He skied down, drove home, and worked out "Annie's Song" on the guitar. The romantic ballad, linking his love for nature and for his wife, turned into a huge international hit.

4 Rocky Mountain High

For a guy who spent his teenage years often in silence with feelings locked inside, music became the key for opening himself to others. He worked hard at relating his ideas and emotions to his audiences, large or small. "I never went out in front of 24 people and did any less of a show than I did in front of 250 people," he told a magazine writer. With the success of "Country Roads," his audiences grew from the hundreds to tens of thousands.

In the introduction to John's autobiography, *Take Me Home*, John's friend and manager Hal Thau described the magnetism between the artist and a concert throng of 18,000 people: "The audience is composed of both men and women, some old, some young, all roaring their approval as the announcer booms through the darkness, 'Ladies and gentlemen, John

Denver!' And then John's voice soars above the din, soothing us and unifying us with his masterful songs. There he is, one man holding the people with the clear, pure sound of his music...people so attentive and so quiet that one can almost hear the proverbial pin drop."

"Brat" Meets "Street Kid"

In 1969, Hal Thau recommended that John get a personal manager to promote his records and concert appearances. One possibility was an aggressive, experienced young promoter named Jerry Weintraub. Hal had doubts about how a Denver-Weintraub team might work. "This meeting may not last three minutes," Thau recalled in an interview, "but I thought I would introduce them."

Weintraub had started working for an artist management company in his early twenties. He handled business details for well-known comedians and music acts. By 1969 at age thirty-two, he had his own company. He managed various performers, including his wife, the famous singer Jane Morgan. Jerry, a feisty "street kid" from New York's Bronx neighborhood, intended to be a powerful force in the entertainment industry.

Courtesy johndenver.com

John substituted Dutch wooden shoes for American cowboy boots on
an early 1970s concert tour in the Netherlands.

Creative sparks flew when the aspiring music star
met the powerhouse manager. Like Batman and
Robin, Denver and Weintraub formed a dynamic duo.

Know More!

Vocal Quality

Throughout John Denver's career, people around the world flocked to his live performances. It was not just his songs that brought them out, it was the way he sang them. What quality in his voice appealed to so many people?

Pete Huttlinger, a musician who accompanied Denver for years, claimed in a video that the "pure honesty" in his voice "was one of his greatest gifts." Annie Denver believed that audiences loved "the crystalline quality" in his voice.

Deborah Jenkins Teske, the conductor of the Colorado Vocal Arts Ensemble, one of Colorado's premier singing groups, is an expert vocal teacher. As a girl, she was also a big John Denver fan. With the skill of a trained musician, she described the quality and appeal of his voice in this way:

John Denver was a tenor who had a voice with no secrets. While his vocal technique was sometimes flawed, he sang with an emotional directness that was undeniable. Contributing to this was his uncommonly clear diction. He sang whole phrases, rather than individual notes. With his lyrics he told whole stories. It is said that the singing voice mirrors the personality. If this is true, then John Denver must have worn his heart unashamedly on his sleeve, embracing life with an honest and forthright passion.

Jerry inspired John's confidence. Their personalities, however, were as different as still water and roaring rapid.

Weintraub planned to boost Denver's image in mid-America first, not on the heavily populated East and West coasts. He described the game plan in this way: "I knew immediately that the **press** would never accept John Denver. There was no glitter, no balloons. It wasn't the Beatles or Elvis. I had a guy singing about mountains, fresh air and his wife. So I said to myself, 'Jerry, let's have a groundswell hero. Let's break him from the heartland and have the people bring him to the press.'"

Hearing "Country Roads" in early 1971, Weintraub grew excited about turning it into a top-selling record. Singer and manager pressed RCA hard to advertise the record far and wide. John hand-carried the single to a radio station in Minneapolis, which began playing it. Soon all the local stations were playing it frequently. More stations in other midwestern cities put the record on their **playlists.** The song's popularity grew until it reached the top of the charts nationwide. Weintraub's game plan had worked.

Eventually, both the "Country Roads" single and the *Poems, Prayers, and Promises* album sold more than one million copies, achieving **platinum record** status in the United States. Hundreds of thousands of listeners in other countries bought the records, too. Today, "Country Roads" is one of the best-known songs in the world.

Far Out in TV Land

Another brilliant Weintraub promotion strategy involved getting John Denver on television. TV programming was conservative in the early 1970s. Channels bringing popular music to television, like MTV or CMT, did not exist. In the opinion of many Americans, rock musicians were out of control both on and off stage. Rock and rollers were said to be drug-crazed and part of a "counterculture," not true American **culture**, and not the kind of people fit for home TV screens.

Denver was different. In fact, he crafted a unique image to present to the public. He described himself this way: "John Denver—this creature of mine—came across very well on the TV screen. Even though I was still one uncertain person, there was something in what I was projecting that held together: the granny glasses, the long hair, the slightly western twang, the sense of humor. Jerry, from the very beginning, touted my down-to-earth unpretentiousness as a quality that people would welcome into their living rooms."

Beginning in 1970, Weintraub landed Denver a number of TV appearances. John played a song and chatted with the **host** on the *Merv Griffin Show* and other talk shows. John hosted the first episode of the pop music show *Midnight Special*, designed to interest young adults in their right to vote. He was a guest on programs with famed comedian Bob Hope and actors Doris Day and Dick Van Dyke. On every show, John found chances to exclaim, "Far out!" Viewers began to identify the John Denver TV "creature" with that expression, whether they felt he was "far out" or not.

Americans celebrated the first Earth Day in April 1970. Concerns for a clean, healthy world flooded newspapers, TV, and people's thoughts and actions. John Denver's musical connection with nature and the outdoors fit right in to the budding environmental movement.

John hosted *Day of the Bighorn*, a documentary about bighorn sheep, filmed in the wilds of Alberta, Canada. Annie joined him for part of the backcountry filming and for the trip back to Colorado. "It was a fabulous drive home," John said, "through rolling hills, and there was even a double rainbow in the sky above us at one point."

Fire in the Sky

Story Behind the Song

In Idaho during the summer of 1971, John helped behind the scenes with the filming of a TV documentary on birds of prey. After memorable experiences handling an eagle, he wrote the high-energy song "The Eagle and the Hawk" for the soundtrack. The music and words combine to express the power and freedom of flight.

Eagles, one of Denver's **totem** animals, appear in several of his songs. In an interview, Annie Denver said, "John always talked about coming back as an eagle" in another life.

"Imagine a moonless night in the Rockies in the dead of summer," John Denver wrote about an August 1971 camping trip with Annie and friends to view the Perseid meteor shower. "*Swoosh*, a meteor went smoking by," he continued. "It got bigger and bigger until the tail stretched out across the sky and burned itself out. It was raining fire in the sky." The impressive meteor show that night deeply impacted John's musical career.

Denver stated, "If my recording of 'Country Roads' made me a star, the recording of 'Rocky Mountain High' gave me superstar status." Magazines started referring to John as "His Rocky Mountain

Courtesy John Stansfield

Two of John Denver's favorite things—music and eagles—are part of this lifesize statue that stands on the grounds of the Windstar Land Conservancy near Aspen.

Story Behind the Song

John took his memories of the meteor-filled night and began work on an autobiographical song. Images of raining fire and tree shadows in starlight stuck with him. It took about nine months to complete "Rocky Mountain High," his song celebrating Colorado and his feelings about living there. The song began:

> *He was born in the summer of his 27th year*
> *Comin' home to a place he'd never been before*
> > *He left yesterday behind him*
> *You might say he was born again*
> *You might say he found a key for every door*
> *And the Colorado Rocky Mountain High*
> *I've seen it rainin' fire in the sky*
> *The shadow from the starlight is softer than a lullaby*
> *Rocky Mountain High . . .*

When the Rocky Mountain High album debuted in 1972, it jumped into the record charts and stayed for five months. In Colorado and many other places, it was hard to turn on the radio without hearing "Rocky Mountain High." The Colorado state legislature designated it as one of the two official state songs in 2007.

Highness." Many people idolized him. Some fanatics took their idol worship too far, sending him weird letters and weirder gifts.

Others strongly disliked the man and his music. Music **critics** labeled John a plastic **Pollyanna**, calling his music "plain as a vanilla milkshake" and his message "Rocky Mountain Hype." Some Coloradans called him "Eco-twerp," claiming he was destroying the state he pretended to love by encouraging too many visitors with his songs. Bumper stickers appeared in Colorado, saying, "John Denver Go Home!" In response to both fawning fans and vocal critics, a sign outside the Denvers' house in Aspen read: "Please don't bother us. You are not welcome here. Thank you!"

Heard Around the World

During the spring of 1973, John starred in a six-week musical **variety program** in the United Kingdom, *The John Denver Show*, aired by the British Broadcasting Corporation. The series featured Bill and Taffy Danoff, a dance troupe, and a top British pop music performer on each program. The show allowed John to learn the skills of hosting a TV program and to build a large UK audience for his music. In the UK, there was, in his words, "less pressure about succeeding than in American television."

While John worked in the UK, Weintraub lined up television **specials** on the ABC network. *The John Denver Special: A Family Event* appeared in 1974, and more shows aired during the next ten years. Huge TV audiences tuned in. Filming the specials took John from Red Rocks outdoor amphitheater in Denver to Australia, New York, Los Angeles, and home to Aspen.

The 1975 special, *An Evening with John Denver,* and the 1976 special, *Rocky Mountain Christmas,* both received Emmy Awards. *Rocky Mountain Reunion* earned six different awards. This 1978 film depicted John and others reintroducing wildlife into native habitats. John hosted the 1976 Emmy Awards show and the recording industry's Grammy Awards programs in 1978, 1979, and 1982.

After the first *John Denver's Greatest Hits* album appeared in 1973, it sold a whopping nine million copies in the United States and hundreds of thousands more in other countries. The record, another example of Weintraub's promotional genius, collected John's limited number of hit songs in one place. Nine albums that followed earned platinum or **gold record** status.

Altogether, an astounding 100 million Denver records were sold during the 1970s. Tracking all the income and paying the sizable bills kept business manager Hal Thau extremely busy.

Television appearances and hit records turned John Denver into the most popular musician in the United States by the mid-1970s. Referring to other famous musicians, record producer Milt Okun said, "What [Frank] Sinatra was to the 1940s, Elvis [Presley] to the 1950s, The Beatles to the 1960s, John Denver was to the 1970s." Among many awards during the decade, John received the Country Music Association's Entertainer of the Year award and the People's Choice Award's Favorite Musical Performer in 1975.

A successful performance often leaves an artist energized. Sometimes after concerts, John and his band and crew celebrated at clubs, drinking a lot. Fans, hungry to meet a favorite star, often joined the party. As a result, John became involved in some short-term romantic relationships that he later regretted.

As John reached heights of fame and wealth, he pondered the future and reflected on the past. In a 1975 magazine interview, he stated, "I've seen success ruin some people and destroy their life and I've been very nervous. But now I look back and see that from my

Denver filmed several TV specials with The Muppets,
including Kermit the Frog.

childhood when I first started singing I have been on

a path that brought me to here. Life is a lot more
demanding right now. There's a lot more that I'm

responsible for, but I am what I've always wanted to be."

Story Behind the Song

Being a celebrity gave John Denver the chance to meet his heroes. Jacques Cousteau, the famed ocean explorer and scientist, was one of them. When John first stepped on the deck of the *Calypso*, Cousteau's ship, the chorus of a new song popped into his head. But throughout the voyage, he made no more progress with the song. Months later, the rest of the song came to him in a flash while skiing. John regularly used the song "Calypso" to give a rousing finish to his concerts.

5 Conundrums

Conundrum Creek tumbles out of the Elk Mountains near Aspen. Close to the creek's high, cold headwaters, steaming hot water springs out of the ground. The contrast of cold and hot waters presents a geological conundrum, meaning a riddle or puzzle difficult to solve. People can face personal conundrums in their lives, too.

The guy who sang so much about home was hardly ever there. In 1976, John Denver was at home in Aspen for only about four weeks. One tour involved concerts in 63 different, far-flung cities in 90 days. While he traveled, Annie often chose to stay home with her friends and life in the mountains.

For John, success was a muscular opponent that presented conflicts between career and family, travel and home. "The difficult thing for us in our life has always been that what I do means as much to me as my family does," he said in a 1976 interview. "I refuse to give either one up for the other." Denver wanted his life both ways. Could it really be that way?

For Annie, her conundrum was being "Mrs. Superstar." "I felt threatened [by John's success], dominated by it. And that scared me," Annie told a newspaper reporter. "Outwardly, I looked fine, but inwardly I was falling into a hole." To climb out, she needed to "get in touch with who I was." Could she move out of John's shadow and claim her own identity?

To deal with their conundrums, John and Annie followed two paths together looking for answers. One way led to Erhard Seminar Training, known as est. The other way led to a son and a daughter.

When est training came to Aspen in 1972, the Denvers joined in. John described his reaction to the seminar: "We found est deeply affecting. I found a framework that allowed me to be more articulate as a person, particularly as it involved feelings." The est experience required speaking out, expressing anger, letting go of personal secrets, and confessing past mistakes.

The training encouraged participants not to be victims of their past. Instead, est pushed them to take responsibility for inner thoughts and feelings and,

Know More!

Inner Space Exploration

In the 1960s and 1970s, astronauts pioneered new frontiers in outer space. At the same time, "inner space" explorers developed programs to help people become more self-aware, happy, and productive at work and play. Some folks found benefit in such "self-help" programs. Others rejected them, believing the programs strayed too far from traditional values.

One such self-help program was est. Founder Werner Erhard based his seminars on ideas found in **psychology, philosophy,** and several religions. Basic est trainings plunged large groups into two-weekend-long psychological "boot camps," led by a demanding instructor. Begun in 1971, est trainings spread rapidly to many cities.

especially, for future actions. Denver claimed, "It was est that gave me the confidence to follow through, eager to do something 'good' in the world. I was going to invest in good works."

John Denver drew his spiritual beliefs from a far-reaching mix of religions and ideas. Est and other practices, including **meditation** and **aikido,** helped Denver control, but not prevent, the emotional waves he rode throughout his life. "John was a real complicated guy," Annie Denver said in an interview. "He had big mood swings. He could be very elated and down in the dumps."

A Sense of Family

After six years of marriage, Annie and John had no children. They both wanted a family. John learned through medical tests that he was **sterile**. After deep discussion, they chose to adopt a child. What race or sex the baby might be did not matter, as long as it was healthy. They applied to a Minnesota adoption agency and waited for word.

The couple traveled to New York City in May 1974, where John performed four sold-out concerts at the huge Madison Square Garden. While in New York, John had a remarkable experience. "I dreamed that three people in white robes came and gave me a boy," he recalled. "It was a dark-faced boy with round eyes and a little bit of an overbite—and as I was holding him, he looked up, grabbed my thumb, and smiled."

Eleven days later, a boy, part Cherokee Indian, was born. The agency told John and Annie the baby would be theirs. Two months later, an adoption worker placed the boy in John's arms. The baby looked just like the one in the dream. When John held him, the boy smiled and took hold of his new father's thumb. From then on, John believed that just as parents choose to have children, children somehow choose their parents. They named the child Zachary John, Zak for short.

Anna Kate came into the Denvers' lives in 1977. The baby, of Japanese and American ancestry, was adopted through the same agency as her brother. Coincidentally, in the fall of 1976, John had returned to Japan for the first time since childhood to perform a series of concerts. The girl and boy brought a great deal of love and joy to their parents.

Even with children to bind them together, the stress of John's career drove wedges into their marriage. *Newsweek* magazine claimed that John was, "the most popular pop singer in America." He worked very hard to maintain that status. In the second half of 1975, for example, he filmed two TV programs—an environmental documentary and the "Rocky Mountain Christmas" special in Aspen—released two record albums, and toured the United States and Australia doing concerts.

Dealing with all that and more, "I was under a lot of pressure," John told *Newsweek*. "I was starting to lose contact with Annie. She wasn't supporting me."

When the couple disagreed, he flew away to Switzerland. "It was only six days," Annie admitted, "but felt like three months." Counseling from friends and tearful phone calls ended the separation. In later years, in spite of working on their problems, the couple agreed to several longer separations.

Investing in Good Works

People recognized John as a **humanitarian** or, in his words, a "world citizen." To John, a world citizen was someone who cared about a healthy planet, its plants and wildlife, and the well-being of all its people. Hundreds of good causes asked Denver for his support and contributions. But just giving money away left him unsatisfied. "If I was going to help," he decided, "I was going to get involved."

Once involved, John was not afraid to be a leader. His good works interested many other people. A friend who worked with him on several community projects remarked: "Whenever you did anything with John Denver, everybody wanted to be involved."

Denver chose his causes carefully. He based his choices on his personal interests and concerns. His work to eliminate world hunger, for example, grew directly out of est. After seeing the documentary film, *The Hungry Planet*, at an est board meeting, John and others volunteered to show and discuss the film with lawmakers and government officials in Washington, D.C. The hunger activists began by seeing John's friend, Senator Wendell Anderson of Minnesota, who had sponsored Zak's adoption. Eventually, they reached all the way to President Jimmy Carter. The message they delivered was that tens of thousands of people worldwide, particularly children, starve to death every day. Yet, our planet grows enough food to feed everyone. We must solve this conundrum.

Two important results emerged from the Washington **lobbying** trip. In 1977, Werner Erhard, college president Robert Fuller, and Denver founded The Hunger Project, a nonprofit group intent on making people aware of solutions for the worldwide problem of **malnutrition** and starvation. And in 1978, President Carter created a 20-person commission to study world and national hunger issues and report their findings.

The president asked John to serve on the hunger commission. Carter said, "While some of us can only reach thousands of people on the problem of hunger, he can reach millions." Also serving on the commission were scientists, businesspeople, educators, senators, and Harry Chapin, another popular singer and songwriter. Active on hunger issues for some time, Chapin co-founded the World Hunger Year organization in 1975. He died in a car accident in 1981. But his group and The Hunger Project remain active today in working to eliminate world hunger.

Despite disappointment that Americans did not take more action on hunger issues, John kept pushing to do what he could. He journeyed to Africa with a Hunger Project group on a fact-finding trip. He wrote a song

Courtesy johndenver.com

A resident of a village in the West African country of
Burkina Faso greets John during a visit in 1983.

entitled "African Sunrise" to describe some of his experiences. In 1985, he received the Presidential World Without Hunger Award from President Ronald Reagan. Over the years, Denver's numerous **benefit concerts** aided groups that promoted peace, children's health, adoption, education, nature conservation, and the elimination of nuclear weapons. He and Jerry Weintraub convinced the ABC network to make a documentary about Alaska's wild lands and its people, with John as reporter. The film, *Alaska: America's Child*, influenced the passage of landmark federal environmental laws at a key moment in the state's history.

Windstar Is Born

Remember the boy in Tucson, swaying in the arms of the eucalyptus tree, dreaming of a place where people could join in conversation and friendship? In 1976, John Denver purchased a 1,000-acre ranch in a shallow valley near Aspen. This place, given the name Windstar, became his long-imagined gathering place.

The concept of Windstar grew from conversations between Denver and friend Tom Crum. An Aspen martial arts master, Crum worked with John on meditation, breathing techniques, aikido, and learning to stay **centered** and strong. During 1970s concert tours, Crum handled security arrangements and, as John stated, helped "me keep my head clear of the chaos."

In his book, *The Magic of Conflict*, Crum called Denver's concerts, "a very powerful demonstration of connectedness." The singer's energy (or *ki*, a Japanese word, as in aikido) radiated out to each audience member. The connection enabled John to enter a

The Windstar property, known as the Windstar Land Conservancy, is home to the Windstar Foundation, the John Denver Meadowlands Open Space, and the Rocky Mountain Institute, an energy conservation and research organization with offices in this solar building.

Story Behind the Song
Genius, inventor, and **visionary** Buckminster Fuller helped shape the Windstar mission. John celebrated his mentor's life in the ballad, "What One Man Can Do." The Denver reggae tune, "World Game," explored Fuller's ideas for making Earth a better place.

stadium and safely perform from a low stage surrounded by a huge audience without security guards nearby. Tom always sat in the front row, just in case.

A rare security incident occurred in Detroit when a large woman managed to reach down from her seat and lift John up by the neck and shoulders. Unable to use his aikido skills, Tom grabbed John's legs and pulled. A moment later, Tom won the tug-of-war, bringing the stretched singer back to earth.

To guide activities at Windstar, Tom and John co-founded the Windstar Foundation, with Crum as director. John called Windstar "a school, meeting place, and model environment combined."

The foundation hosted children's nature day camps, adult seminars, films, and lectures exploring many environmental topics. From 1986 to 1995, people from

Courtesy John Stansfield

Erma and Ron Deutschendorf pose in front of a John Denver memorial quilt during the 2006 Windstar Symposium at Snowmass, Colorado.

around the world gathered to share important ideas at the Windstar Symposium. Windstar's role as a "model environment" took two forms, earth-friendly agriculture and renewable energy projects. Today, Windstar continues under the leadership of John's brother, Ron.

While Windstar fulfilled John's lifelong dream, the foundation often created financial nightmares. Carrie Click, a former employee, told a reporter that in the late 1980s, John "was writing a very substantial check every month to keep it afloat." Denver stated that to support his good works, "I needed to take home more than $2 million a year."

Forest Conservation

Continuing his good works, John founded Plant-It 2000 (now Plant-It 2020) in 1992. The organization's goals are to plant, maintain, and protect native trees worldwide. With more than five million trees planted since its founding, Plant-It 2020 continues Denver's vision that forests, like oceans, form the heart of a healthy Planet Earth.

John viewed creating Windstar and Plant-It 2000 as some of the most positive achievements of his life. When asked what one individual can do about huge environmental problems, he stated in a video, "You don't have to do it all. You do the thing you can do. I'll do the thing I can do. We'll try to get these other people to do what they can do and we can save ourselves."

One Who Wanted To Fly

While flying from Dayton, Ohio, to Minneapolis after a concert one starkly clear night, the pilot invited John into the jet's cockpit. Below, stretched out along the edge of Lake Michigan, the lights of several cities shone like necklaces glittering at the lakeshore's dark throat.

The sight filled John with wonder. "My responses," he said, "told me that flying was something I had in my blood."

Shortly afterward, John began taking flight lessons in a small propeller aircraft. When Dutch, now retired from the Air Force, heard the news, he gladly volunteered to continue his son's instruction. In the experience of flying together, John noted with satisfaction, "We found our way to a relationship between father and son that seemed to work for the first time."

His demanding travel schedule dictated that Denver buy a jet. Dutch became his pilot. Teaching his son to pilot the Lear jet one day, Dutch put John through all kinds of imaginary in-flight emergencies. John tried to follow Dutch's rule: make the plane do what you want it to do. When John landed the jet, he was tense and soaked with sweat. Dutch congratulated him with a pat on the shoulder and a proud, gleeful smile. It was the kind of approval that John had always looked for from his father but rarely received.

6 Returning to Earth

John Denver's flying ambitions soared from jets to outer space. *The Higher We Fly*, his 1980 TV special on the history of flight, allowed him to fly everything from antique planes to a space shuttle simulator. After rigorous training, he was accepted as an astronaut for the proposed Citizens in Space program. He lost his chance at space flight when the program focus changed to Teacher in Space. For his strong support of the U.S. space program, John received the Distinguished Public Service Medal from NASA, the U.S. space agency, in 1985.

On January 28, 1986, teacher Christa McAuliffe and six other crew members on the space shuttle *Challenger* lifted off into the sky. In only 73 seconds, their journey ended in a tremendous explosion. Their shattered ship and dreams fell back to earth. Watching

Story Behind the Song
John dedicated "Flying for Me" from his *One World* album to the *Challenger* crew and other astronauts. In the song's chorus, he wrote:

> *They were flying for me*
> *They were flying for everyone*
> *They were trying to see a brighter day for each and everyone*
> > *They gave us their light*
> > *They gave us their spirit and all they could be*
> *They were flying for me*

news coverage of the *Challenger* disaster, Denver realized he could have been onboard.

Oh, God

Building on his success in TV, Denver yearned to act in movies. Jerry Weintraub was anxious to expand from music promoter to motion picture **producer**. They both found a pathway to movieland in the 1977 comedy, *Oh, God*. John starred as Jerry Landers, an assistant grocery store manager amazed one day to meet God, played by the elderly comedian George Burns.

In the film, God informs Jerry, "I set the world up so it can work. And you're my messenger." The messenger must tell everyone to take care of each other and all creation. Being messenger to the world on screen and through music was fine with John Denver. "I feel that that's my role," he told a magazine interviewer. "I feel I'm a messenger."

George Burns, with his ever-present cigar, laughs with John on the set of the movie Oh, God.

Oh, God was a big hit with the public. Many film critics praised John's acting. Weintraub became a powerful player in the film industry. He produced many more movies, but, to John's regret, never another feature film project for his client.

The Missing Man

After his retirement, Dutch Deutschendorf piloted airfreight planes for a while. Then he and Erma settled in Aurora, Colorado. He headed Windstar Aviation, taking care of John's aircraft and training pilots to fly them. With his son's encouragement, Dutch started shaping up. He watched his diet, exercised, and gave up one of his favorite habits, drinking alcohol.

Despite Dutch's healthier lifestyle, he had bouts of serious illness, including pneumonia. Following the illness, he decided to enjoy himself, and took up drinking alcohol again. In March 1982, he attended one of John's concerts in Lake Tahoe, Nevada. After returning home, he had a massive heart attack and died at age 61. At his burial, Air Force jets passed overhead in the "missing man" formation. The V-shaped cluster left a space empty for one plane, representing the dead pilot.

Falling Out of Marriage

The year 1982 was a hard one for John Denver's emotions and self-confidence. Three months after Dutch's death, Annie asked John for a divorce on their fifteenth wedding anniversary. Disappointments, disagreements, and separations had taken their toll on the marriage. Annie had moved herself off "the back burner," as she put it. No longer just "Mrs. Superstar," she had grown comfortable with herself and with setting her own goals.

The divorce did not surprise John. Still, he grieved the loss of his wife and best friend. He struggled through a range of emotions—first, a feeling of numbness, then anger at being deserted. Ultimately, he accepted the reality that in the conflict of career and family, one side must lose. With time and their shared role as parents, John said, "Annie and I even reestablished our friendship."

Demise of the Dynamic Duo

Like his marriage to Annie, John's relationship with Jerry Weintraub lasted 15 years. The extremely successful business partnership came crashing down in 1984.

During an ugly confrontation in Los Angeles, John fired his personal manager.

Denver's complaints about Weintraub were many. He broke promises to find John more feature and TV movie roles. Weintraub had Milt Okun fired as John's record producer. And John said Weintraub put his own interests first. Most of all, Denver had lost trust in his longtime friend.

Weintraub reacted by threatening to sue Denver for breaking their contract. Hal Thau, however, kept John's best interests at heart. As he writes in his book, *Bronx to Broadway*, Thau had lawyers develop a fourteen-page-long list of ways Weintraub had broken his contract with John. When John promised to countersue for $100 million, Weintraub dropped his legal threat.

A Record Breakup

John Denver's fans around the world continued to support him during the 1980s. He had no top-ten hits. Except for a few songs, he got little radio airplay. But people filled arenas wherever he performed. They bought his records in large numbers, though not as many as in the 1970s. RCA Records paid him a $1 million advance for each album. The songs he recorded during that period were about love and losing love, flying, and his concerns for peace, freedom, and wild places.

Times were changing at RCA and in the music world. RCA was sold twice, and new managers changed the company's musical priorities. In 1986, after twenty-five albums, RCA released its best-selling artist for financial reasons. John was like a famous, but high-salaried baseball player let go by his team. It took two years for John to put out his next album. *Higher Ground* was released on his own Windstar label.

Man for the World

China's vice-premier Deng Xiaoping made his government's first visit to the United States in 1979. President Carter invited John Denver and other entertainers to present a concert for the special visitor. John introduced "Country Roads" with a few halting Chinese phrases. His music and words impressed Deng greatly. After the concert, Milt Okun learned that Deng wanted hundreds of cassette tapes of John's music to take back to China. Okun arranged the shipment.

Know More!

Cold War

In 1945, the Allied Forces, led by the Soviet Union, Great Britain, and the United States, defeated the Axis powers of Germany, Italy, and Japan to end World War II. Instantly, the **Cold War** broke out among the Allies. The Eastern Bloc countries, particularly the Soviet Union and China, used the economic and social systems of **communism**. They wrestled for world domination with the Western Bloc countries, led by the United States and Great Britain, which used **capitalism** as an economic system and **democracy** in government.

Competing in a fast-growing arms race, the Cold War opponents built huge stockpiles of nuclear bombs, missiles, and other weapons. They held enough firepower to destroy all life on Earth. Each side restricted the free flow of travel, business, and culture to the other side. After more than 40 years, the Cold War ended with the collapse of the Soviet Union. China continues to use a communist system, now infused with some capitalist economic policies.

Two years later, Denver traveled to China as a tourist, not a performer. In Shanghai, Okun said in an interview, "Dozens of people started gathering and pointing, 'John Denver, John Denver.' And he couldn't quite understand it. Turns out the [vice-premier] had sent the cassettes to all the radio stations in China, who weren't given permission to play western music, except for this."

After his father's death and his divorce, John felt a desire for global travel with a purpose. "The world was opening for exploration in a way that hadn't been possible for a long time," he said. "I thought that, given my celebrity as a singer and songwriter, I might be able to do something to further the cause of East/West understanding."

Denver longed to open a doorway to peace with the Soviet Union. A program allowing artists' visits between the United States and Soviet Union had ended in 1980. John pulled lots of strings in Washington and Moscow, getting permission for a visit. The singing goodwill ambassador made several Soviet tours in the 1980s.

Story Behind the Song

In 1984, John visited a cemetery in Leningrad in the Soviet Union. There he saw the graves of hundreds of thousands who had died in the German siege of the city during World War II. The experience moved him to write "Let Us Begin." The song, about the horrible waste created by war, asks, "What are we making weapons for?" He recorded the song in Moscow with famed Russian singer Alexander Gradsky. Denver believed the song and its stark music video was some of his best work.

Audiences often sang his songs with him in English, and he sang some in Russian.

Despite John's popularity in China, it took him until 1992 to became the first Western performer to tour there. In China and wherever Denver went in the world, he took photographs. His sharp eye captured detail in wild nature, architecture, and in people. His photos, like his music, often highlighted human qualities shared by people around the world.

Love Again and Disappointment

A young woman wearing white crossed the busy lobby of an Australian hotel. Seeing her, John Denver was struck by her beauty. She soon disappeared in the crowd, but the next day she sent John a telegram with her name and phone number, followed by a packet of promotional material on herself. She was Cassandra Delaney, an Australian singer and actor.

Accompanied by her mother, Delaney met Denver after his 1986 concert in Sydney. The couple grew close during the rest of his stay in Australia. When John returned to Aspen, Cassandra, seventeen years younger than John, was with him. Her mother and friends expressed grave concerns about her hasty decision. Cassandra would not change her mind.

Cassandra sang with John on a European tour that summer. "The thing I loved about Cassandra," John said, "was that she came on the road with me, not just that once, but time after time. I know she was after something: first to marry me, and beyond that to further her career. I was supporting that, too." The couple married August 12, 1988, in an Aspen mountaintop ceremony.

Although John had been told he was sterile, the newlyweds held "fantasies about having a family." They tried new medical treatments and spiritual exercises. To their amazement, Cassandra became pregnant shortly after the wedding. Jesse Belle, their daughter, was born in May 1989, with John assisting Cassandra during the birth.

Despite a period of joy after their daughter's birth, Cassandra and John did not stay married long. "Cassie

Story Behind the Song
John dedicated his 1990 album, *The Flower That Shattered the Stone*, to Jesse Belle. It contains three songs about being born into a new, sometimes uncertain world.

Courtsey johndenver.com

John holds daughter Jesse Belle at an event a few months after her birth.

and I," John confided, "never discussed how we'd live *after* Jesse's birth." The two strong-willed people headed off in different directions. Their divorce turned into an expensive, emotional mess.

Still, Cassandra told an Australian magazine that after signing the divorce papers in August 1993, they hugged and went out for dinner and a bottle of wine. That night, police arrested John for drinking and driving. Exactly one year later, John crashed his vintage yellow Porsche near his home, splitting open his forehead. After a trip to the hospital, he was arrested again for drunken driving. Long, complicated legal proceedings followed the second arrest.

Like his father, John enjoyed alcohol. The problem was the amount he sometimes drank, especially during periods of stress and depression. A **thyroid condition**, affecting how quickly he digested food and drink, may have worsened his problem with alcohol.

Climbing Down the Mountain

Hal Thau cleverly described John Denver's later career when he wrote: "This is the period that is difficult for a lot of entertainers who have done well. They have

Story Behind the Song

In *The Wildlife Concert*, John premieres his expertly written "A Song for All Lovers." The ballad tells the story of conservationists Olaus and Mardy Murie and their love for each other and for Alaska. John treasured that state's vast wild country, its wildlife, and its pioneering residents, like the Muries. He wrote songs about Alaska and visited there several times for both work and recreation.

climbed a mountain, and now they are on the other side having to climb down, and the two journeys are not equivalent."

Following his second divorce, Denver struggled to stay motivated and positive. Thau, now John's personal manager and artistic cheerleader, encouraged him to write and practice new songs. He fretted over John's whining long-distance calls complaining about minor tour details. What drove the manager crazy was the singer—rich and admired as he was—pitifully "crying woe is me" in interviews.

After 30 years of tiresome touring, John Denver, the musician, was still masterful. His audiences' applause told him so. As did some significant awards, which recognized the value of his artistic and humanitarian work:

the Albert Schweitzer Music Award in 1993, named for the famous musician and pioneering missionary doctor in Africa; and induction into the Songwriters Hall of Fame in 1996.

A superb example of John's later work was the 1995 *The Wildlife Concert*, a combination live performance, TV special, DVD with interview, and double CD, all benefiting the Wildlife Conservation Society. John and his crew worked for months to produce a high-quality package.

In the concert interview, John reaffirmed his lifelong belief in human equality and the power of music:

John gathers with his children, Anna Kate, Jesse Belle, and Zak.

"Music does bring people together. It allows us to experience the same emotions. No matter what language we speak, what color we are, the form of our politics, or the expression of our love and faith, music proves: we are the same."

Epilogue

In Greek mythology, Daedalus was a renowned inventor and craftsman. Imprisoned on an island with his son Icarus, Daedalus crafted wings from feathers, wax, and string. Father and son flew away from the island toward freedom. But in his love of flight, Icarus soared too high above the cool ocean. The sun melted the wax in his wings, and he plunged to his death in the sea.

Sunday, October 12, 1997, started as a good day for John Denver. He played golf with friends in scenic Monterey, California. Golf was only one of John's recreational passions. He also loved skiing, hiking, horseback riding, and, especially, flying. According to friends and relatives, John's life was on an upswing. His relations with ex-wife Cassandra were improving. He had bought a house in the Monterey area to be closer to daughter

Jesse Belle. And the day before, he had picked up a new airplane, an experimental Long-EZ.

That Sunday evening, Denver inspected the plane and took off on a short flight. After practicing three "touch-and-go" landings at the airport, he headed west over the ocean. Witnesses on the beach reported hearing a "pop" or "backfire" and reduced engine noise. The plane then banked steeply right and plunged nose-down into the sea, about 150 yards from shore. Medical reports indicate that John, in falling from the sky like Icarus, probably died instantly on impact with the water. He was 54 years old.

People around the world and especially in Colorado responded to the news of John's death with the sorrow of loss and the joy of remembrance. His friend Tom Crum stated at the memorial service, "I am sorry that he died, but I am so very, very happy that he lived." An overflow crowd of more than 2,300 people attended the memorial service in Aurora, near his mother's home. The following day, another 1,200 celebrated his life in Aspen. In many other places, indoors and outdoors, people held celebrations of Denver's life.

In Aspen each October, people from far and near gather for John Denver Week. Most of the events focus on revisiting John's life and music, in the place he loved.

As Ron Deutschendorf stated at his brother's memorial, "John is here with us. Anytime you go out in these hills, he'll be around."

In tribute to his life and musical legacy, Hal Thau produced the stage musical, *Almost Heaven: The Songs of John Denver*. The show has been performed in Denver, New York, and other cities.

As for John's own sense of his contribution to the world, two years before his death he said in an interview: "I would most like to be remembered for the fact that I stood up for what I believe in. That I spoke for it. I sang for it. I worked for the things I believe in, in the world."

Shortly after the death of his father in 1982, John wrote "On the Wings of a Dream." The song ponders life, death, and what might come after death. Written in memory of his father, "On the Wings of a Dream" is perhaps a fitting memorial for the songwriter himself:

From the life to the light
From the dark of the night to the dawn
He is so in my heart
  He is here he could never be gone
  Though the singer is silent
There still is the truth of the song
  Yesterday I had a dream about dying

About laying to rest and then flying
How the moment at hand is the only thing we really own
   And I lay in my bed and I wonder
   After all has been said and is done for
   Why it is thus we are here
   And so soon we are gone

Courtesy John Stansfield

Large stones carved with the words to a number of John Denver's songs grace a sanctuary in his honor, which sits on the banks of the Roaring Fork River in downtown Aspen.

Timeline

1943 — Henry John Deutschendorf is born on December 31 in Roswell, New Mexico.

1943–1963 — Deutschendorf family lives in New Mexico, Oklahoma, Japan, Arizona, Alabama, and Texas.

1961 — John Deutschendorf graduates from Arlington Heights High School, Fort Worth, Texas, and enrolls at Texas Tech University.

1964 — Leaves Texas Tech and goes to Los Angeles, California, to begin a professional music career. Hired at Ledbetter's club and takes the stage name of John Denver.

1965 — Plays extended engagements at the Jester club in Houston, Texas, and the Lumber Mill club in Scottsdale, Arizona. Hired for the Mitchell Trio.

1966 — Meets Ann Martell after a spring concert in Minnesota and begins courting her in fall.
Writes the future hit song, "Leaving on a Jet Plane." Makes first of three records with the trio.

1967 — Marries Ann Martell on June 9. Honeymoons in Europe, location of a failed Mitchell Trio tour. "Leaving on a Jet Plane" is recorded by Peter, Paul, and Mary. Decides to pay back the Mitchell Trio's $40,000 debt.

1968 — Tours with David Boise and Mike Johnson after Mitchell Trio dissolves.

1969 — Performs solo after trio breaks up. Sees "Leaving on a Jet Plane" reach number one on record charts. Signs contract for four records with RCA. Records first solo album, *Rhymes and Reasons*. Hires personal manager Jerry Weintraub.

1970 — Visits Aspen with Annie, where they pick out a lot in Starwood for a future home. Writes "Take Me Home, Country Roads" with Bill and Taffy Danoff.

1971 — Records *Poems, Prayers and Promises* album containing "Country Roads," which goes platinum and launches his national fame. Writes music for TV wildlife special and begins writing "Rocky Mountain High."

1972 — Records *Rocky Mountain High* album, which goes platinum. Hosts TV wildlife special. Takes est training with Annie in Aspen.

1973 — Records *John Denver's Greatest Hits*, which sells more than any other record in the decade. Hosts musical variety TV series in the United Kingdom. Contracts for TV specials with ABC. Begins pilot training with his father and others.

1974 — Presents first ABC-TV special. Records another platinum album, *Back Home Again*. Tours extensively. Adopts Zachary John Deutschendorf.

1975 — Releases three albums. Hosts two TV specials. Tours for concerts in the United States and Australia. Wins several important music and television awards. Separates briefly from Annie.

1976 — Purchases Windstar property outside Aspen. Travels at home and abroad (including Japan) for concerts, recording, and TV production for almost eleven months.

1977 — Stars in the movie *Oh, God.* Lobbies for hunger prevention in Washington, D.C. Helps found the Hunger Project. Adopts Anna Kate Deutschendorf. Receives the designation Poet Laureate of Colorado.

1978 — Hosts the award-winning wildlife documentary, *Rocky Mountain Reunion.* Tours Australia and makes a TV special there. Serves on President's Commission on World Hunger.

1979 — Records and films for TV the special, *A Christmas Together,* with Jim Henson's Muppets in London. Films the TV documentary *Alaska: America's Child* during summer. Founds Windstar Foundation with Thomas Crum.

1980 — Hosts and flies in a TV documentary on the history of flight, *The Higher We Fly.*

1982 — Mourns the death of his father in March and the end of his marriage to Annie in June. Stars with The Muppets on the TV special and album *Rocky Mountain Holiday.*

1984 — Ends his business relationship with manager Jerry Weintraub.

1985 — Tours the Soviet Union giving concerts. Receives the Distinguished Public Service Medal from NASA and the Presidential World Without Hunger Award from President Reagan.

1986 — Hosts the first Windstar Symposium, which continues until 1995. Ends his relationship with RCA Records after 25 albums. Stars in TV movie *The Christmas Gift*. Begins a relationship with Australian singer Cassandra Delaney.

1987 — Stars in the TV movie *Foxfire*.

1988 — Stars in a TV movie set in Alaska, *Higher Ground*, and releases his first album on the Windstar Records label. Marries Cassandra Delaney on August 12 in Aspen.

1989 — Assists at the May birth of daughter Jesse Belle.

1992 — Performs in Communist China, the first American artist to do so. Founds Plant-It 2000.

1993 — Receives the Albert Schweitzer Music Award. Ends his marriage to Cassandra.

1995 — Stars in the multimedia production, *The Wildlife Concert*.

1996 — Inducted into the Songwriters Hall of Fame.

1997 — Stars in the feature film *Walking Thunder*. Dies in a plane crash near Pacific Grove, California, on October 12, 1997.

2007 — The Colorado legislature adopts "Rocky Mountain High" as one of two official Colorado state songs.

New Words

acoustic — instruments that produce sound without being electrified

aikido — a martial art, founded in Japan, whose purpose is to resolve physical conflict by making an attack harmless without harming the attacker

architecture — the profession of designing buildings, open spaces, communities, and other things that are constructed by humans

benefit concerts — performing arts events put on to raise money and support for a cause, usually a person or nonprofit organization in need of help

boycotted — refused to have contact or do business with another person, company, or government with whom someone disagreed

bribes — a valuable item given or promised to tempt a person to do something illegal or unfair

capitalism — an economic system in which land and natural resources, manufactured goods and services, and the exchange of money are made mostly by competing private individuals and companies, not by governments

centered — a balance of mind, body, and spirit connecting humans through alertness and the senses to the world around them

civil rights — the rights to equal legal, social, and economic opportunity provided to all individuals and groups in a country

cold war — a conflict fought mostly with military threats, as well as economic, cultural, and political tactics, rather than a war involving violent conflict

communism — a political system in which government controls economic activity and civil rights, while holding all property in common for citizens

courtship — the persuasive wooing, or courting, of one person by another for the purpose of establishing a personal relationship

critics — a person, often a newspaper, magazine, or Web log writer, skilled in judging the qualities of literature or an artistic performance

culture — human activities involving visual arts, performing arts, language arts, and literature

democracy — government in which power is wielded directly by the people or by their elected representatives

draftsman — a person employed to make drawings of machines, plans, or designs

equality — the state of being equal, as in having equal rights for all people

folk music — music of a simple style from cultures worldwide, often handed down orally

gig — an opportunity to perform before an audience, often for pay

gold record — in the United States, a recording that sells more than half a million copies

harmony — playing or singing notes simultaneously that form a musical chord and sound pleasing to the ear

headliner — a performer who is the top or featured artist among others working at the same place

hootenanny — an informal gathering at which folk musicians share songs with each other

host — a person who acts as host for a show, introducing entertainers, while often also performing as part of the program

humanitarian — a person who helps improve the welfare and happiness of humanity

lobbying — trying to directly influence the votes of lawmakers on certain proposals

malnutrition — lack of proper food supply, causing insufficient or unbalanced nutrition

meditation — quiet, solitary thought or contemplation

military regimen — a strict code of behavior administered to keep discipline in the military

patter — the conversation or story that a musician shares with an audience between songs

philosophy — the study of the truths and principles of knowledge, conduct, and reality

platinum record — in the United States, a recording that sells more than one million copies

playlists — limited lists of music chosen to be played at any one time by broadcasters, usually radio stations

Pollyanna — an extremely optimistic person

press — a general term for the news media, including newspapers, television, radio, and others

producer — a person responsible for the financing and administration of a play, film, television, or radio production

protest songs — music, often in the folk music style, that raises objections to injustices in a society

psychology — the study of human and animal behavior

repertoire — the list of pieces that a performing artist is prepared to play

royalties — a part of the income, usually a fixed percentage, from a musical composition paid to the composer

satire — a composition using humor, sarcasm, ridicule, and other techniques to criticize foolish, illegal, or immoral behavior

segregation — the forced separation of one group from another, often for racial or religious reasons

social activist — a person who works to protect equality or eliminate injustice in a society

specials — one-of-a-kind programs, usually on television, that are not part of a regular series

sterile — incapable of producing children

tenor — the male singing voice higher than bass and baritone

thyroid condition — a problem with the function of the thyroid gland, which regulates body growth and the processing of food

totem — an animal or object to which a person feels closely related

troubadour — a wandering singer or minstrel

tsunami — an unusually large sea wave produced by an underwater earthquake or volcanic eruption

variety program — a performance featuring different art forms, such as music, dance, and comedy

visionary — a person who speculates realistically or imaginatively on what the future holds

Sources

Aspen Times, December 27–28 , 1997.

Australian Women's Day, November 17, 1997.

Collis, John. *John Denver: Mother Nature's Son*. Edinburgh and London: Mainstream Publishing, 1999.

Crum, Thomas F. *The Magic of Conflict: Turning a Life of Work into a Work of Art*. New York: Simon and Schuster, 1987.

Denver, John. *Take Me Home: An Autobiography*. With Arthur Tobier. New York: Harmony Books, 1994.

Minneapolis Star and Tribune, June 18, 1982.

National Transportation Safety Board Report, Identification number LAX98FA008.

Newsweek, December 20, 1976.

People, February 26, 1979.

Playboy, December 1977.

Rocky Mountain News, October 18, 1997.

Rolling Stone, May 8, 1975.

Saturday Review, July–August, September–October, 1985.

Thau, Harold. *Bronx to Broadway: A Life in Show Business*. With Arthur Tobier. New York: Applause Theatre and Cinema Books, 2002.

Time, October 17, 1978.

VIDEO

A Song's Best Friend: John Denver Remembered. New York: Sony BMG Music Entertainment, 2005.

John Denver: A Portrait. New York: Cherry Lane Video, Inc., 1994.

John Denver: The Wildlife Concert. New York: Legacy, 1995.

WEB SITES

John Denver The Rocky Mountain High Fan Club
www.shellworld.net/~emily/
With many links to articles and information about John Denver

JohnDenver.com
www.johndenver.com
The official Web site of John Denver.

Plant-It 2020
www.plantit2020.org
Current activities and history of the nonprofit tree-planting organization
founded by John Denver in 1992.

Sing365.com
www.sing365.com
Lyrics for John Denver songs.

The Windstar Foundation
www.wstar.org
Current activities and history of Windstar.

The World Family of John Denver
www.john-denver.org
Information and many links to John Denver

www.youtube.com (A John Denver search on the video streaming site
YouTube returns about 3,900 results)

Index

Acknowledgments

An African proverb says that a person is never really dead until he or she is forgotten. The life and accomplishments of John Denver are kept alive through the work of many people who contributed to this book. Librarians at the Pitkin County Public Library, the Denver Public Library Western History Department, and the Colorado Historical Society Hart Library provided assistance with research materials. The Hart Library archive also provided photos. Bonnie Barnes helped give direction to the research. Thomas Crum contributed valuable source material. Harold Thau was gracious in providing commentary and text review, as well as photographs. Through the *Now You Know Bio* book series, Doris Baker and the staff of Filter Press keep alive the stories of remarkable Coloradans whose life stories should never be forgotten.

Research for this book was made possible by a grant from Colorado Humanities, Denver, Colorado, and the National Endowment for the Humanities. Any views, findings, conclusions, or recommendations expressed in this publication do not necessarily represent those of the National Endowment for the Humanities or Colorado Humanities.

About the Author

For more than thirty years, storyteller and author John Stansfield has recounted stories of notable people from Colorado history. His book *Writers of the American West: Multicultural Learning Encounters* (Teacher Ideas Press, 2002) earned a Colorado Authors' League Award and was a finalist for the Colorado Book Award. He previously wrote *Enos Mills: Rocky Mountain Naturalist* (Filter Press, 2005) for the *Now You Know Bio* series. Stansfield presents a one-man show reenacting the life of Enos Mills. He teaches storytelling as a member of the adjunct faculty of the University of Colorado–Colorado Springs.

John spends his spare time working to protect Colorado's wild places. For these efforts, the Wilderness Society presented him an Environmental Heroes Award in 2004. He and his wife, Carol, live in Larkspur, Colorado, on the high divide between the South Platte and Arkansas Rivers at the foot of the Rocky Mountains.

John Stansfield
PO Box 588
Monument, CO 80132
jorcstan@juno.com